JOSEPH MIDTHUN   SAMUEL HITI

BUILDING BLOCKS OF SCIENCE

MATTER

and its properties

WORLD
BOOK

a Scott Fetzer company
Chicago

www.worldbook.com

World Book, Inc.
233 N. Michigan Avenue
Chicago, IL 60601
U.S.A.

For information about other World Book publications, visit our website at http://www.worldbook.com or call 1-800-WORLDBK (967-5325).

For information about sales to schools and libraries, call 1-800-975-3250 (United States); 1-800-837-5365 (Canada).

Library of Congress Cataloging-in-Publication Data

Matter and its properties.
     p. cm. -- (Building blocks of science)
  Includes index.
  Summary: "A graphic nonfiction volume that introduces the properties of matter. Features include several photographic pages, a glossary, additional resource list, and an index"--Provided by publisher.
  ISBN 978-0-7166-1429-6
  1. Matter--Properties--Juvenile literature. I. World Book, Inc.
QC173.16.M38 2012
530--dc23
                              2011025905

Building Blocks of Science
Set ISBN: 978-0-7166-1420-3 (print, hc.)

Also available as:
ISBN: 978-0-7166-1471-5 (pbk.)

E-book editions:
ISBN 978-0-7166-1868-3 (EPUB3)
ISBN 978-0-7166-1447-0 (PDF)

Acknowledgments:
Created by Samuel Hiti and Joseph Midthun.
Art by Samuel Hiti. Written by Joseph Midthun.

© Dreamstime 8; © istockphoto 11; © Shutterstock 8, 9, 10; © FoodCollection/SuperStock 11; WORLD BOOK illustration by Linda Kinnaman 24-25.

Printed in China by Leo Paper Products, LTD., Heshan Guangdong
3rd printing June 2014

ATTENTION, READER!

Some characters in this series throw large objects from tall buildings, play with fire, ride on bicycle handlebars, and perform other dangerous acts. However, they are CARTOON CHARACTERS. Please do not try any of these things at home because you could seriously harm yourself—or others around you!

STAFF
Executive Committee
President: Donald D. Keller
Vice President and Editor in Chief: Paul A. Kobasa
Vice President, Sales & Marketing: Sean Lockwood
Vice President, International: Richard Flower
Director, Human Resources: Bev Ecker

Editorial
Manager, Supplementary Publications: Cassie Mayer
Writer and Letterer: Joseph Midthun
Editors: Mike DuRoss and Brian Johnson
Researcher: Annie Brodsky
Manager, Contracts & Compliance (Rights & Permissions): Loranne K. Shields

Manufacturing/Pre-Press/Graphics and Design
Director: Carma Fazio
Manufacturing Manager: Steven Hueppchen
Production/Technology Manager: Anne Fritzinger
Proofreader: Emilie Schrage
Senior Manager, Graphics and Design: Tom Evans
Coordinator, Design Development and Production: Brenda B. Tropinski
Book Design: Samuel Hiti
Photographs Editor: Kathy Creech

TABLE OF CONTENTS

There is a glossary on page 30. Terms defined in the glossary are in type **that looks like this** on their first appearance.

The ground under your feet is made of matter.

The water in a river is made of matter.

The clouds above you are made of matter.

The stars in the sky are made of matter.

Even *you* are made of matter.

Matter is anything that has **mass** and **volume**.

MEASURING MATTER

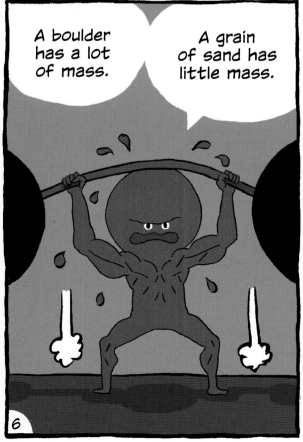

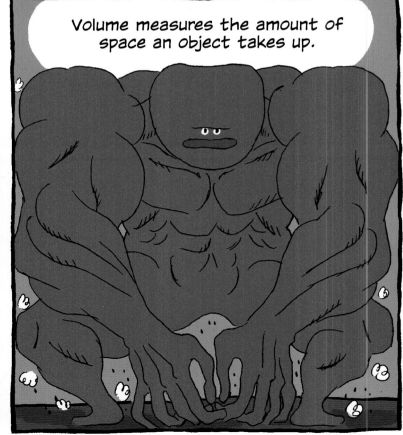

For example, take a bowling ball and a balloon.

The bowling ball has more mass than the balloon.

But they both take up about the same space.

They have similar volume. How can this be?

The bowling ball packs more mass into the same amount of space.

This is called **density**.

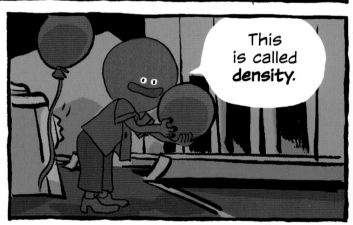

Density measures how much matter is in a certain space.

The bowling ball is more dense than the balloon.

Strike!

SWOOP

CRASH

PROPERTIES OF MATTER

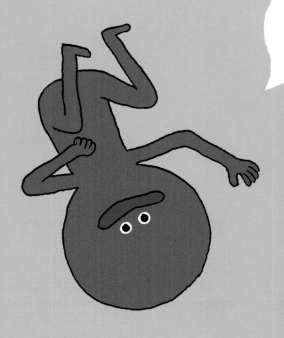

Mass, volume, and density are **properties** of matter.

Properties of matter can be used to describe objects.

COLOR

TEXTURE

SHAPE

SIZE

These pages show examples of some properties of matter you can see or feel.

...if it dissolves in a liquid.

...how easily it melts, freezes, or changes into a gas.

A LOOK INSIDE

But what is matter *really* made of?

Let's take a look inside!

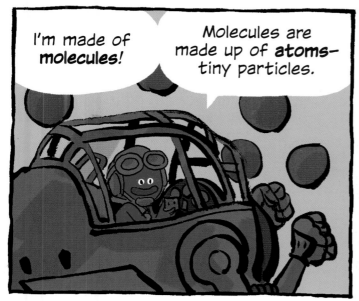

I'm made of **molecules!**

Molecules are made up of **atoms**— tiny particles.

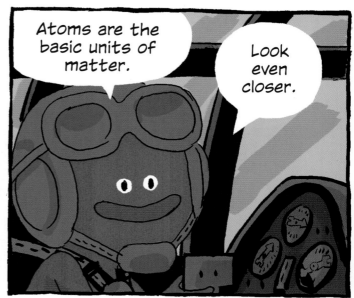

Atoms are the basic units of matter.

Look even closer.

Atoms have a **nucleus,** or center.

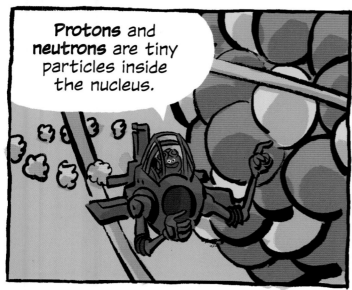

Protons and **neutrons** are tiny particles inside the nucleus.

Electrons are even tinier particles that move around the nucleus.

ELEMENTS AND COMPOUNDS

So if all matter is made of atoms, why are there different kinds of matter? It has to do with protons.

Atoms can have different numbers of protons. For example, hydrogen is the smallest atom. It has only one proton.

Oxygen is a bigger atom. It has eight protons.

The number of protons determines the type and size of an atom.

An **element** is another word for a substance with only one type of atom.

Like an ingredient!

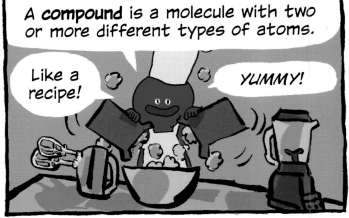

A **compound** is a molecule with two or more different types of atoms.

Like a recipe!

YUMMY!

Let's start with an atom of oxygen.

Oxygen is an element.

Add two atoms of the element hydrogen.

Mix them up and...

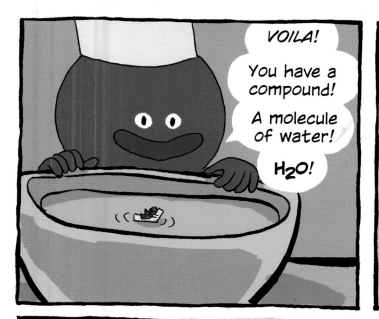

VOILA!

You have a compound!

A molecule of water!

H_2O!

Atoms, molecules, elements, and compounds are the building blocks of the world we live in.

But as you may have noticed, matter doesn't always look the same.

Matter can have different forms.

They're called the **states of matter!**

STATES OF MATTER

Matter can be a solid, a liquid, or a gas.

In a solid, the molecules move *SLOWLY*.

Solids have a set volume and shape.

In a liquid, the molecules move *FASTER*.

SLURP

Liquids move freely and take the shape of whatever container they are in.

But their volume stays the same.

In a gas, the molecules move the *FASTEST*.

Sphiss

Gases have no shape of their own.

They can **expand** or **contract** to fill almost any space.

Their volume can change.

So what causes matter to change states?

ENERGY!

Energy has the ability to cause change.

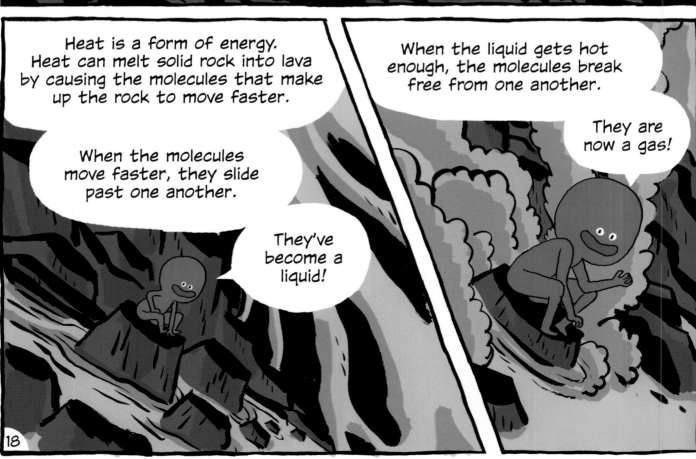

Heat is a form of energy. Heat can melt solid rock into lava by causing the molecules that make up the rock to move faster.

When the molecules move faster, they slide past one another.

They've become a liquid!

When the liquid gets hot enough, the molecules break free from one another.

They are now a gas!

Watch what happens when I toss this giant ice cube into a volcano.

WOOSH

SPLOOSH

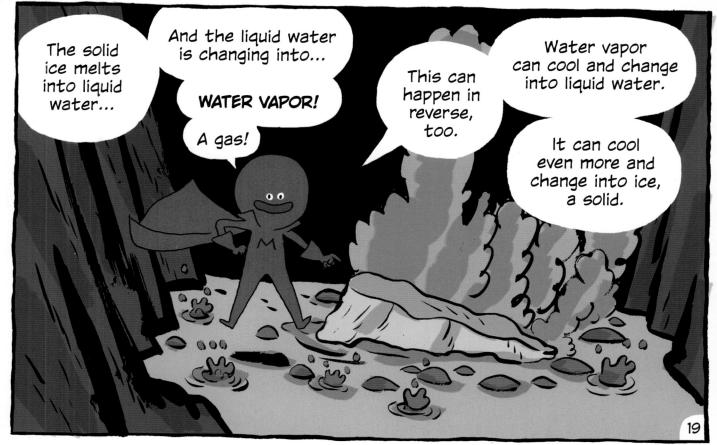

The solid ice melts into liquid water...

And the liquid water is changing into...

WATER VAPOR!

A gas!

This can happen in reverse, too.

Water vapor can cool and change into liquid water.

It can cool even more and change into ice, a solid.

As you have seen, not all matter is the same.

Scientists group almost all elements of matter into two categories:

Metals and **nonmetals**.

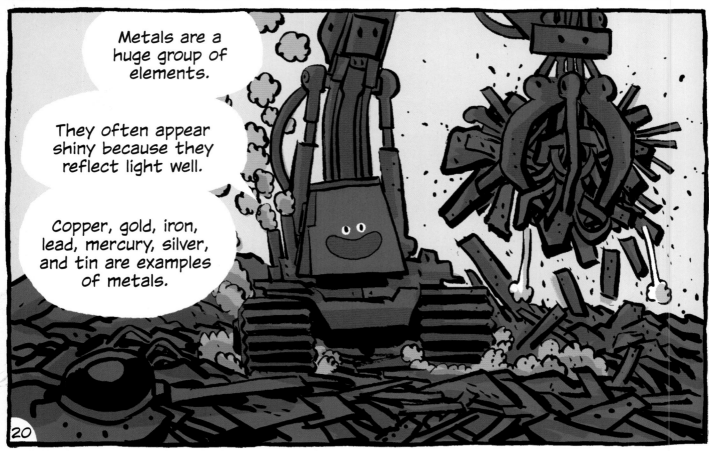

Metals are a huge group of elements.

They often appear shiny because they reflect light well.

Copper, gold, iron, lead, mercury, silver, and tin are examples of metals.

All metals are solids at room temperature *except* mercury, which is a liquid.

The atoms in most metals are closer together than the atoms in nonmetals.

This makes metals more dense.

HOP

Metals can be shaped into useful objects.

They can be hammered into thin sheets without breaking.

They can be drawn into wires.

Most metals are also good **conductors** of heat and electricity.

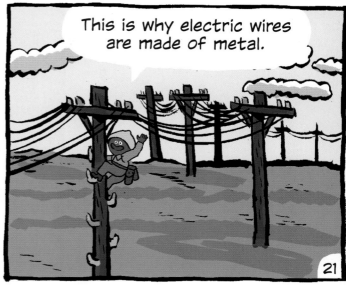

This is why electric wires are made of metal.

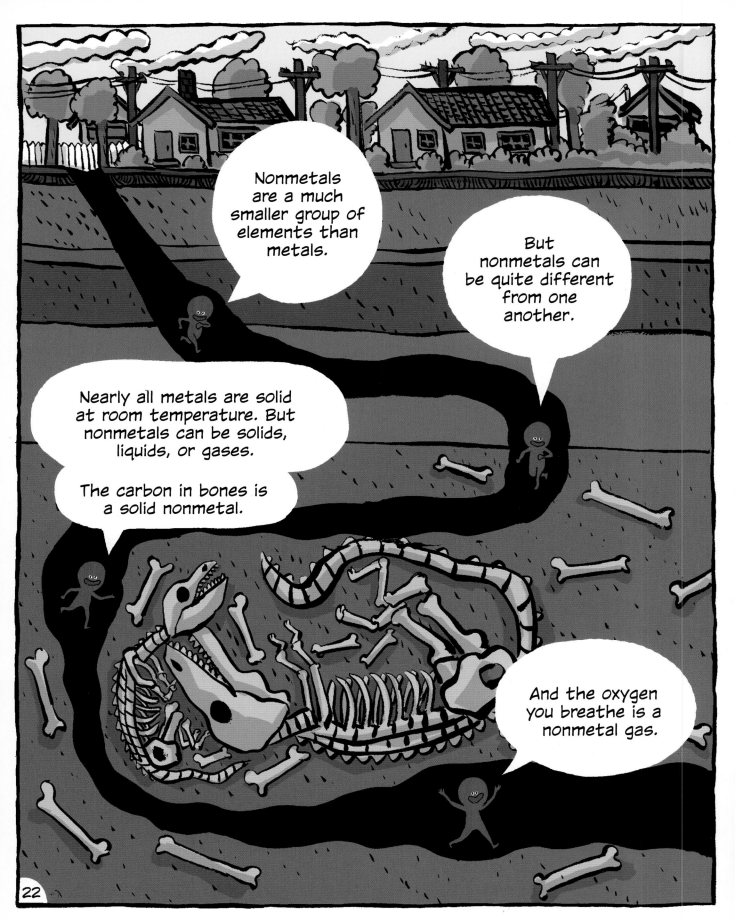

Nonmetals generally do not conduct heat or electricity well.

Almost all solid nonmetals are brittle and break easily.

They cannot be shaped.

snap

Nonmetals usually appear dull, but they have a wider range of colors than metals.

So how can we figure out which elements are metals and which elements are nonmetals?

THE PERIODIC TABLE

The **periodic table** lists all the elements that scientists have identified so far.

Metals are on one side of the table and nonmetals, except hydrogen, are on the other side.

Each element has its own symbol. Remember when we made a molecule of water?

I called it H_2O.

Here's why!

You can read the table like this...

1								
1 **H** Hydrogen	2							
3 **Li** Lithium	**4** **Be** Beryllium	3	4	5	6	7	8	9
11 **Na** Sodium	**12** **Mg** Magnesium							
19 **K** Potassium	**20** **Ca** Calcium	**21** **Sc** Scandium	**22** **Ti** Titanium	**23** **V** Vanadium	**24** **Cr** Chromium	**25** **Mn** Manganese	**26** **Fe** Iron	**27** **Co** Cobalt
37 **Rb** Rubidium	**38** **Sr** Strontium	**39** **Y** Yttrium	**40** **Zr** Zirconium	**41** **Nb** Niobium	**42** **Mo** Molybdenum	**43** **Tc** Technetium	**44** **Ru** Ruthenium	**45** **Rh** Rhodium
55 **Cs** Cesium	**56** **Ba** Barium		**72** **Hf** Hafnium	**73** **Ta** Tantalum	**74** **W** Tungsten	**75** **Re** Rhenium	**76** **Os** Osmium	**77** **Ir** Iridium
87 **Fr** Francium	**88** **Ra** Radium		**104** **Rf** Rutherfordium	**105** **Db** Dubnium	**106** **Sg** Seaborgium	**107** **Bh** Bohrium	**108** **Hs** Hassium	**109** **Mt** Meitneriu

57 **La** Lanthanum	**58** **Ce** Cerium	**59** **Pr** Praseodymium	**60** **Nd** Neodymium	**61** **Pm** Promethium	**62** **Sm** Samarium	**63** **Eu** Europiur
89 **Ac** Actinium	**90** **Th** Thorium	**91** **Pa** Protactinium	**92** **U** Uranium	**93** **Np** Neptunium	**94** **Pu** Plutonium	**95** **Am** Americiu

Atomic Number
Atomic Symbol
Atomic Name

1
H
Hydrogen

The symbol for hydrogen is *H*— get it?

"H" for hydrogen.

"O" for oxygen.

So the symbol for a molecule of water, two hydrogen atoms and one oxygen atom, is H_2O!

			13	14	15	16	17	18
								2 **He** Helium
			5 **B** Boron	6 **C** Carbon	7 **N** Nitrogen	8 **O** Oxygen	9 **F** Fluorine	10 **Ne** Neon
10	11	12	13 **Al** Aluminum	14 **Si** Silicon	15 **P** Phosphorus	16 **S** Sulfur	17 **Cl** Chlorine	18 **Ar** Argon
28 **Ni** Nickel	29 **Cu** Copper	30 **Zn** Zinc	31 **Ga** Gallium	32 **Ge** Germanium	33 **As** Arsenic	34 **Se** Selenium	35 **Br** Bromine	36 **Kr** Krypton
46 **Pd** Palladium	47 **Ag** Silver	48 **Cd** Cadmium	49 **In** Indium	50 **Sn** Tin	51 **Sb** Antimony	52 **Te** Tellurium	53 **I** Iodine	54 **Xe** Xenon
78 **Pt** Platinum	79 **Au** Gold	80 **Hg** Mercury	81 **Tl** Thallium	82 **Pb** Lead	83 **Bi** Bismuth	84 **Po** Polonium	85 **At** Astatine	86 **Rn** Radon
110 **Ds** Darmstadtium	111 **Rg** Roentgenium	112 **Cn** Copernicium	113 * **Unutrium**	114 **Fl** Flerovium	115 * **Ununpentium**	116 **Lv** Livermorium	117 * **Ununseptium**	118 * **Ununoctium**

*Atomic symbol to be determined

64 **Gd** Gadolinium	65 **Tb** Terbium	66 **Dy** Dysprosium	67 **Ho** Holmium	68 **Er** Erbium	69 **Tm** Thulium	70 **Yb** Ytterbium	71 **Lu** Lutetium
96 **Cm** Curium	97 **Bk** Berkelium	98 **Cf** Californium	99 **Es** Einsteinium	100 **Fm** Fermium	101 **Md** Mendelevium	102 **No** Nobelium	103 **Lr** Lawrencium

Metals   Metalloids   Nonmetals

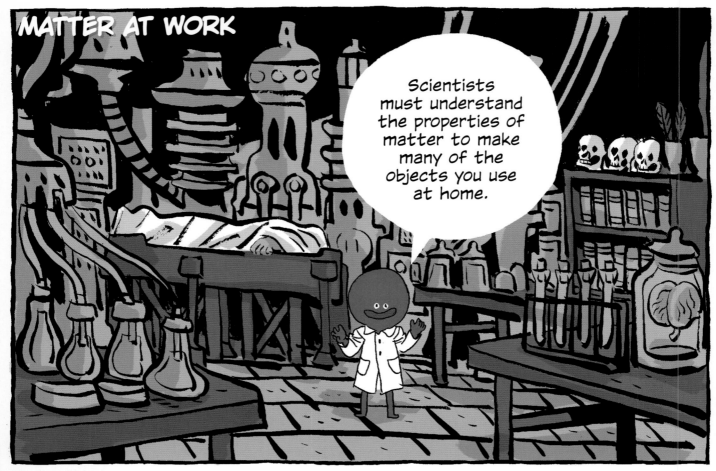

YUM

YUM!

YUM!

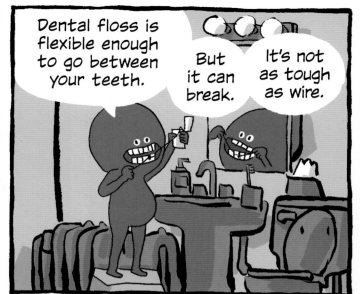

Dental floss is flexible enough to go between your teeth.

But it can break.

It's not as tough as wire.

Wires are made of metal.

zap zap zap

Metals are good conductors of electricity.

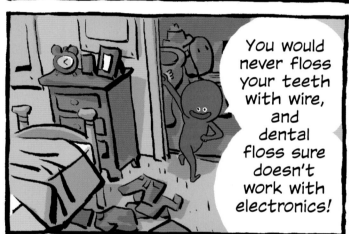

You would never floss your teeth with wire, and dental floss sure doesn't work with electronics!

Without an understanding of the properties of matter, you wouldn't be able to make anything!

GLOSSARY

atom one of the basic units of matter.

attract to pull one object toward another.

compound a substance that contains more than one kind of atom.

conductor something that allows heat, electricity, light, sound, or other form of energy to pass through it.

contract to decrease in size.

density the amount of matter in a particular volume of a substance.

electron a kind of particle that circles around the nucleus (center) of an atom. Electrons have a negative electric charge.

element a substance made of only one kind of atom.

expand to increase in size.

mass the amount of matter in an object.

matter what all things are made of.

metal any of a large group of elements that includes copper, gold, iron, lead, silver, tin, and other elements that share similar qualities.

molecule Two or more atoms chemically bonded together.

neutron a kind of particle inside the nucleus (center) of an atom. Neutrons have no electric charge.

nonmetal materials that do not have the properties of metals. Wood, glass, plastic, and rock are examples of nonmetals.

nucleus the center of an atom. Protons and neutrons are inside the nucleus.

periodic table a chart that lists the known chemical elements arranged according to their characteristics.

property quality or power belonging specially to something.

proton a kind of particle inside the nucleus (center) of an atom. Protons have a positive electric charge.

states of matter the different forms of matter. The most familiar are solid, liquid, and gas.

volume the amount of space something takes up.

water vapor water in the state of a gas.

FIND OUT MORE

Books

Change It! Solids, Liquids, Gases and You by Adrienne Mason and Claudia Davila (Kids Can Press, 2006)

Matter by Christopher Cooper (DK Publishing, 1999)

Mixtures and Compounds by Alastair Smith, Philip Clarke, and Corinne Henderson (Usborne, 2002)

Physics: Why Matter Matters! by Dan Green and Simon Basher (Kingfisher, 2008)

Science Fair Projects About the Properties of Matter: Using Marbles, Water, Balloons, and More by Robert Gardner (Enslow Publishers, 2004)

Science Measurements: How Heavy? How Long? How Hot? By Chris Eboch and Jon Davis (Picture Window Books, 2007)

Touch It! Materials, Matter, and You by Adrienne Mason and Claudia Davila (Kids Can Press, 2005)

What Is Matter? by Don L. Curry (Children's Press, 2004)

Websites

The Atom Builder
http://www.pbs.org/wgbh/aso/tryit/atom/
The tiny, mighty atom is made up of even smaller parts! Build your own atoms at this website from PBS's A Science Odyssey.

The Atoms Family
http://www.miamisci.org/af/sln/
Learn about the basic building blocks of matter—atoms—at this educational site from the Science Learning Network.

Chem4Kids: States of Matter
http://www.chem4kids.com/files/matter_states.html
Learn more about the states of matter at this fun and educational chemistry site.

Little Shop of Physics
http://littleshop.physics.colostate.edu/amazingphysics.htm
At this website, you will find experiments in force, energy, and motion, along with other basic physics concepts.

Marvelous Molecules
http://www.nyhallsci.org/marvelousmolecules/
Check out this website for activities and information about the molecules that make up the world around us.

The Particle Adventure
http://particleadventure.org/
Explore the fundamentals of matter and force at this educational website from the Particle Data Group.

Strange Matter
http://www.StrangeMatterExhibit.com/
What makes up all the things around us? What makes different materials so different? Find out more about matter and materials at this website.

INDEX